ANIMAL GYMNASTICS

Isabel Thomas

capstone®

Edited by Linda Staniford
Designed by Steve Mead
Picture research by Kelly Garvin
Production by Victoria Fitzgerald
Originated by Capstone Global Library Ltd
Printed and bound in China

19 18 17 16 15
10 9 8 7 6 5 4 3 2 1

Library of Congress Cataloging-in-Publication Data
Cataloging-in-publication information is on file with the Library of Congress.
Written by Isabel Thomas
ISBN 978-1-4109-8093-9 (hardcover)
ISBN 978-1-4109-8101-1 (eBook PDF)

Acknowledgments
The author and publisher are grateful to the following for permission to reproduce copyright material: Getty Images: Al Tielemans/Sports Illustrated, 14, Martin Harvey/Gallo Images, 5, Popperfoto, 6, 10, Thomas Coex/AFP, 18; Minden Pictures: Gavin Maxwell, 27, Shinichi Takeda/Nature Production, 12; National Geographic Creative/Tim Laman, 23; Newscom: Cede Prudente/NHPA/Photoshot, 16, David Eulitt/MCT, 4, Hiroya Minakuchi/Minden Pictures, 21, Sergei Ilnitsky/EPA, 22, Stephen Dalton/NHPA/Photoshot, 13; Shutterstock: Ahuli Labutin, 9, AndreAnita, 25, fototehnik, 7, michael sheehan, 24, 31; Superstock: Cusp/Cusp, 8, Minden Pictures, 17, NaturePL, 11, NHPA, 18-19; Wikimedia/Ingo Rechenberg, 20

Artistic Elements: Shutterstock: kavalenkava volha, Kozoriz Yuriy, La Gorda, Nikiteev_Konstantin, PinkPueblo, Potapov Alexander, yyang

We would like to thank Michael Bright for his help in the preparation of this book.

Every effort has been made to contact copyright holders of any material reproduced in this book. Any omissions will be rectified in subsequent printings if notice is given to the publisher.

All the Internet addresses (URLs) given in this book were valid at the time of going to press. However, due to the dynamic nature of the Internet, some addresses may have changed, or sites may have changed or ceased to exist since publication. While the author and publisher regret any inconvenience this may cause readers, no responsibility for any such changes can be accepted by either the author or the publisher.

007494CTPSS16

Key₀

 Mammals

 Birds

 Fish

 Reptiles and Amphibians

 Invertebrates

CONTENTS

Some words are shown in bold, **like this**. You can find out what they mean by looking in the glossary.

LET THE GAMES BEGIN!

Every four years, the Olympic Games test the speed, skill, and strength of the world's best athletes. In gymnastics, **competitors** score points for perfect balance, **coordination**, and control.

In any forest, ocean, or grassland, you'll find animals that could rival the best human gymnasts. Balance and coordination are **adaptations** that help animals to **survive**. Let's find out which animal gymnasts deserve a medal at the Animalympics!

BALANCE BEAM

Gymnasts have 90 seconds to leap, turn, and somersault along a beam as wide as their hand! Difficult moves win extra points. This is a test of balance, where one wobble means disaster.

balance beam

🐻 Squirrels

For squirrels, great balance brings a reward: food. A squirrel's long tail is adapted to help it balance while climbing and leaping from tree to tree.

Female squirrels have longer tails. This gives them the extra balance they need when they are carrying a baby.

Tarantula

A tarantula's skeleton is on the outside, making it very fragile. Good balance helps it **survive**. Some scientists think tarantulas use tiny threads of sticky silk to help them climb jungle trees.

short, powerful legs

🐻 Mountain goat

Mountain goats can balance on narrow ledges and perform daring leaps. Their hooves are adapted to grip the rock like the soles of climbing shoes. Each hoof is split into two "toes," which spread out to help the goat brake, or squeeze together to grip tiny bumps in the rock.

Climbing skills allow mountain goats to live out of the reach of hungry bears and mountain lions.

VAULT

Gymnasts use the vault to launch themselves into the air. Before they land, they must fit in as many somersaults, twists, and turns as possible. The springboard helps gymnasts to change a fast sprint into a powerful jump. Humans are not the only animals that use springs to help them jump higher.

vault

London 2012

Colobus monkey

Colobus monkeys use flexible branches as springboards. They jump down on a branch, which springs back and launches them back up into the air. This helps them leap between trees 20 feet (6 meters) apart, and to escape from hungry, heavier **predators**, such as chimpanzees.

tail used for balance and steering

Tree frog

In order to jump high, animals need to push against the ground with as much **force** as possible. Some animals have developed an amazing **adaptation**— a built-in springboard! A tree frog's long legs act like catapults, storing energy slowly and releasing it in one huge burst.

By storing energy before they jump, some tree frogs can boost their muscle power by seven times.

 # Flea

Fleas also make super spring-loaded jumps. Catches lock their legs in place as a springy pad inside each leg is slowly squeezed. When the catches are released, the pad springs back to its normal size. All the stored energy goes to the flea's toes, launching the flea high into the air.

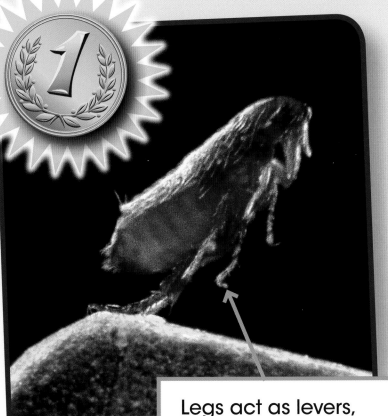

Fleas can jump more than 200 times their body length, onto the large animals they live and feed on!

Legs act as levers, transferring all the stored energy to the flea's toes.

UNEVEN BARS

Gymnasts soar between the uneven bars, scoring points for different grips, flips, twists, and turns. The bars can be up to 6 feet (1.8 meters) apart, so this event tests timing and **coordination**.

top bar

lower bar

Flying snake

In tropical rain forests, flying snakes take a shortcut from tree to tree. Instead of slithering across the ground, they glide between branches up to 98 feet (30 meters) apart!

Flying snakes flatten the base of their bodies into a shape like a bird's wing. This shape helps to slow their fall.

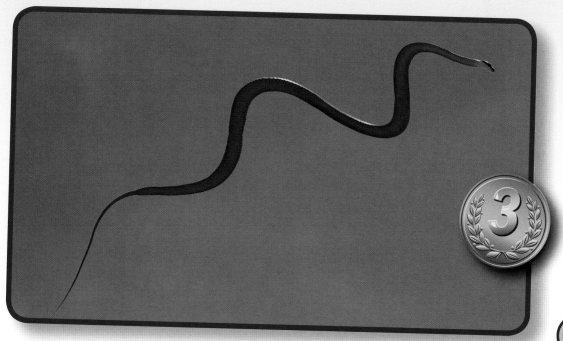

🐻 Flying lemur

Imagine placing the uneven bars at either end of a football field. No problem for flying lemurs! These tiny mammals can glide about 330 feet (100 meters) between branches. All four feet land at once, earning top scores for **coordination**.

thin skin acts like a parachute

Amazing eyesight helps these **nocturnal** animals make perfect landings in the dark.

🐻 Gibbon

Gibbons swing through forests arm over arm, flying up to 32.8 feet (10 meters) between branches. Their bodies are so well adapted that swinging uses less energy than walking from tree to tree—and allows gibbons to move at up to 30 miles (50 kilometers) per hour.

long arms

Traveling by swinging is called brachiating. It helps gibbons gather food over a large **territory**.

FLOOR EXERCISE

The floor is a springy square where gymnasts prove their bodies are strong and flexible. They have to perform acrobatic moves forward, backward, and sideways! Can any other animals keep up?

A bouncy floor helps gymnasts spring more than 6.5 feet (2 meters) high.

Tree lizards

Lizards such as the leaf-tailed gecko are great gymnasts, leaping from branch to branch to escape danger. Lizards can shed their tails if they are grabbed by a **predator**— an **adaptation** that helps the lizard **survive**, but messes up their jumping ability.

Scientists found that a missing tail can mean lizards perform backflips every time they try to leap!

tail provides balance

Moroccan flic-flac spider

Meet a spider that moves like a gymnast! The flic-flac spider cartwheels and backflips up and down desert sand dunes. This helps it escape danger twice as fast as running.

The spider was named after the "flic-flac," or back handspring.

🐻 Dusky dolphin

Dolphins leap from the water to spin, twist, and somersault in the air. Dusky dolphins have been seen performing the same **sequence** 36 times in five minutes!

Splashing noises may help dolphins confuse fish, and make the fish easier to catch. But some scientists think that dolphins somersault to communicate with other dolphins—or just for fun!

RHYTHMIC GYMNASTICS

Rhythmic gymnasts perform graceful routines with ropes, hoops, balls, clubs, and ribbons. They have to keep the **apparatus** moving, while leaping, balancing, and pivoting on the floor.

ribbon

body makes a flowing shape

Bird of paradise

Male birds of paradise have feathers three times as long as their bodies—like the ribbons used by gymnasts. They get in the way as the bird feeds and flies, but they help the birds to attract mates.

Tail feathers fall off and grow back every year.

The long ribbons tell females that the male must be strong and healthy, if he can carry around huge feathers he doesn't need!

Dung beetle

Rhythmic gymnasts perform with a soft rubber or plastic ball that weighs at least 14 ounces (400 grams). This may not impress a dung beetle, which can control a ball of dung 50 times heavier than its body!

The beetles shape dung into balls so that they can roll it to a safe place. Later, they'll eat it or lay eggs inside.

Red-crowned cranes

Cranes win gold for their acrobatic dances. As the birds pair up to **breed**, they bow, spin, leap, and flap their wings in perfect time with their partner. Red-crowned cranes even toss sticks high into the air, just like a gymnast with clubs!

Some cranes dance for up to four hours. The graceful moves help a pair of birds to bond for life.

AMAZING ADAPTATIONS

Animals don't show off their strength, balance, and skill as a sport. The body features that make animals good at swinging, leaping, or balancing are **adaptations** that help animals **survive** in certain **habitats**.

These features help animals to find food, attract mates, care for their young, or avoid getting eaten. This means they will get passed on to the next **generation**.

Watching record-breaking animal gymnasts helps scientists find out how animal bodies work. This information is used in amazing ways.

The amazing eyesight of jumping spiders is being used to improve 3-D cameras.

MEDAL TABLE

It's time for the Animalympic medal ceremony! The animal kingdom is divided into groups. Animals with similar features belong to the same class. Which class will take home the most medals for gymnastics?

 ## Mammals

Mammals are warm-blooded animals with hair or fur that feed milk to their young. They live on the land and in water, and range in size from a bumble-bee-sized bat to the blue whale, the largest animal on Earth!

 ## Reptiles and Amphibians

Reptiles and amphibians are cold-blooded animals, which means they rely on the Sun's energy to stay warm. Reptiles have dry, scaly skin. Amphibians have moist, smooth skin.

 ## Birds

Birds have feathers, wings, and a beak. Most birds can fly, and some can do incredible acrobatics in the air.

 ## Invertebrates

This group includes all animals without a backbone, such as insects, spiders, and snails. Many have a skeleton on the outside of their bodies instead.

 ## Fish

Fish live in saltwater or freshwater. They have fins for swimming and gills to breathe underwater.

RESULTS

EVENT	③ BRONZE	② SILVER	① GOLD
BALANCE BEAM	Squirrel	Tarantula	Mountain goat
VAULT	Colobus monkey	Tree frog	Flea
UNEVEN BARS	Flying snake	Flying lemur	Gibbon
FLOOR EXERCISES	Tree lizard	Moroccan flic-flac spider	Dusky dolphin
RHYTHMIC GYMNASTICS	Bird of paradise	Dung beetle	Red-crowned crane

ANIMAL	RANK	GOLD	SILVER	BRONZE
Mammals	1	①①①	②	③③
Invertebrates	2	①	②②②	
Birds	3	①		③
Reptiles and amphibians	4		②	③③
Fish	5			

GLOSSARY

adaptation change to the body or behavior of a type of living thing that makes it better suited to its habitat

apparatus equipment used by gymnasts when they perform

breed mate with another animal to produce offspring (babies)

competitor person taking part in a sports match or contest

coordination using different parts of the body together, smoothly, and in time

force push or a pull

generation group of living things that were born, or are living, at the same time

habitat place where a plant or animal lives

nocturnal active at night

predator animal that hunts and kills other animals for food

sequence set of moves, performed in the same order each time

survive stay alive

territory area of land defended by an animal or group of animals

FIND OUT MORE

Books
de la Bédoyère, Camilla. *Could a Shark Do Gymnastics?*
   Irvine, Calif.: QEB, 2015.

Morey, Allan. *Gymnastics* (Summer Olympic Sports).
   Mankato, Minn.: Amicus, 2016.

Murphy, Julie. *Amazing Animal Adaptations* series.
   Mankato, Minn.: Capstone, 2012.

Internet sites
Facthound offers a safe, fun way to find Internet sites related to this book. All of the sites on Facthound have been researched by our staff.

Here's all you do:
Visit www.facthound.com
Type in this code: 9781410980939

INDEX